Achievable Dreams

Achievable Dreams

SMART INVESTING
FOR YOUR FUTURE

Steven T. Cox, CFA®

ACHIEVABLE DREAMS
Smart Investing for Your Future

Copyright © 2024 by Steven T. Cox

All scripture quotations, unless otherwise marked, are taken from the English Standard Version (ESV).

Interior Layout and Design by Stephanie Anderson
Book Cover Design by Abigael Elliott

ISBNs:
979-8-89165-171-5 *Paperback*
979-8-89165-172-2 *Hardback*
979-8-89165-170-8 *E-book*

Published by:
Streamline Books
Kansas City, MO
streamlinebookspublishing.com

STREAMLINE
BOOKS

This book is dedicated to my wife of thirty-eight years, Beth, who has encouraged me through my dreams. She was instrumental in building a strong foundation for our sons during my years of travel, and she has been a constant support as I embarked on my dream of having my own firm.

CONTENTS

INTRODUCTION

On many occasions, I've had new clients apologize to me for having what they perceived as a modest investment portfolio, and they questioned whether their portfolio even met the minimum criteria for my assistance. They've said things to me like, "I'm not sure if I have enough money or assets to even plan for retirement." However, once I actually delved a bit deeper into their financial circumstances, I usually uncovered some surprising revelations, and we discovered that they actually had access to more money than they realized.

It's common for people who are not extremely affluent to assume that their financial holdings and investments are too meager to plan for a comfortable retirement, but the truth is, many of them have accumulated a far more substantial amount of money than they knew. And when I finally bring together all of their financial resources and show them the big picture of their financial situation, they're amazed. That's when they say, "Wow, I didn't realize I was in such a great position to plan for the future!"

A recent example involved a lady from my church and her spouse, each of whom had earned an annual income of $50,000 over the years. Despite never reaching a six-figure taxable income and having never consulted with a financial advisor, the couple, in their early seventies, sought our guidance. Understandably, they came to my firm with reservations. They weren't sure if they had too little to fund their retirement or if it was too late to come up with enough money.

Honestly, even I had some initial reservations about the adequacy of their financial portfolio, but it soon became clear during our discussion that they had acquired over $400,000 from various places throughout their years. On top of that, I was impressed to discover that they were entirely debt-free.

The couple had simply never consolidated their financial assets, so they didn't realize how much they had or how well they were positioned for retirement. It was only when they first contemplated a visit to our office that they began to bring together all of the pieces of their overall financial picture. During our meeting, they discovered that they were in excellent financial shape, with more than enough savings to maintain their current lifestyle in retirement, despite their advanced age.

Although initially apologetic for not having a larger sum to invest, they collaborated with me to create a retirement budget tailored to their needs. The realization that they could comfortably retire with financial security, even though they were already in their seventies, transformed their initial nervousness into contentment by the time they left my office. It's a scenario I've seen many times.

In my experience, many people underestimate the true potential of their financial resources to provide for their retirement. They are convinced that their investment capacity is too limited. The same might be true of you. Is it possible that you have underestimated just how much potential you have for creating a comfortable retirement lifestyle?

This is one reason the role of an advisor is so important, particularly an advisor who is not selling specific financial products but rather focusing on planning and investment.

Common Scenarios

There are two common scenarios that frequently unfold when people seek my guidance. First, like the couple from church, many discover that their financial standing is more substantial than they initially thought. Second, many people have not yet thoroughly assessed their spending habits or considered how they're going to finance their retirement, so they don't know what's possible. And sometimes, both scenarios are true at the same time.

In another instance, a couple in their mid-fifties came to me with a lot of uncertainty about what kind of retirement lifestyle they could achieve. Despite their relatively younger age, the woman hoped to retire by age sixty-five, and possibly sooner, so they both maintained a frugal lifestyle. The woman worked a full-time job, the man engaged in contract work, and they owned some inherited assets. When we totaled all of their financial assets from every source, they discovered that they had almost $500,000 available to them.

Utilizing our planning software, we meticulously input their goals, which included her desire to take cruises and his interest in going on mission trips. By consolidating all their financial components—expenses, savings, projected Social Security benefits—we outlined a comprehensive plan that would provide enough money during retirement to fund these endeavors.

This holistic approach to their retirement plans revealed that not only could they comfortably retire at sixty-five, but with further consideration of health care options, an even *earlier* retirement was also a distinct possibility. They were both amazed to learn that their dreams were already within their reach!

That is the essence of what a competent advisor has to offer. Our role is to bring together all the financial facets of a person's life to discover what is possible and achievable. Some clients find the numbers intimidating, but our expertise lies in demystifying financial complexities. Clients may approach us with apologies, fear, or uncertainty about their retirement prospects, so our aim is to identify the financial components, provide clarity, and guide them through the emotional aspects associated with retirement.

It's a bit like fixing an old car that's suffering from vapor lock. If you're old enough, you might remember that older-model cars with carburetors were highly susceptible to vapor lock, which occurred when the fuel became too hot and vaporized. This caused a disruption in fuel flow, which made the engine stall.

Some of our clients come to us with so much anxiety, uncertainty, and confusion about retirement planning that they're struggling to make decisions. It's a kind of emotional vapor lock. We aim to cool down their financial concerns, fine-tune the necessary components, and ultimately leave our clients content with their retirement outlook.

But Why Write a Book?

The truth is, I never set out to write a book. It wasn't one of my career goals or a personal ambition. And writing this book wasn't simply some kind of marketing tactic. Actually, a friend encouraged me to write it. Seeing the common challenges that my clients face and recognizing my extensive and diverse experience within the investment sphere, he approached me and urged me to share my insights on navigating this complex landscape with a broader audience. So here we are.

I took on this project with the hope of aiding and serving readers the same way I serve clients every day. It's my desire that readers of this book—people just like you—will ultimately learn that, irrespective of your current position in investments or your lifestyle goals, there are a few specific aspects of retirement planning that are absolutely vital to your long-term success, and they merit your focus and attention.

I'm not trying to cause apprehension by pointing out all of the things you need to get done or overwhelm you with a bunch of tasks and homework. Rather, my intention is to encourage you to start setting goals for your future and leveraging your financial achievements to your own benefit.

At the same time, I want to demystify the intricate world of investing, alleviating the fear that often accompanies important financial considerations. Building an investment portfolio can seem overly complex if no one has ever sat down with you and explained how to approach it, so we'll spend some time doing just that.

Many people get nervous when talking about retirement planning because they're afraid they're going to have to change their lifestyle and cut way back in order to retire comfortably. Interestingly, this concern is more prevalent among the affluent than individuals with more modest financial means. I intend to assist you in confronting this fear by aiding you in navigating the complexities of lifestyle changes. Planning for a comfortable retirement lifestyle in the future doesn't require you to live a miserable life of deprivation now.

Many people also get nervous at the possibility of depleting their financial resources too fast and no longer being able to afford their desired lifestyle. I hear it all the time: "How can I make sure

I don't run out of money during retirement?" I'm not going to pretend like this never happens. If you don't plan well, you can indeed spend too much too quickly during retirement and find yourself facing lean years. But it doesn't have to be that way as long as you plan well for your future income needs.

From an investment standpoint, these are the two primary fears I consistently encounter: fear of lifestyle changes now and fear of running out of money later. The root cause of both of these fears is confusion and a lack of understanding regarding financial matters. I'm going to try to bring some clarity to the subject so you can practice informed decision-making with clear goals and a real understanding of your options when planning for retirement. If I achieve that in this book for even a handful of people, then it will have been well worth my time to write and publish it.

The Road Ahead

Of course, the end goal of all of this is to help you comprehend the intricacies of constructing a well-rounded investment portfolio that will provide for your future needs. To that end, we're going to delve into the investment strategies that possess enduring value and longevity, distinguishing them from higher-risk alternatives.

To be clear, it's not possible to cover every single investment opportunity out there because there are countless stocks, bonds, mutual funds, real estate properties, and alternative investments you could purchase. However, I intend to provide enough of an overview that you will get a good "lay of the land," and at the very least, you'll know where to start looking.

We're going to explore the process of shaping your current financial position to lay the groundwork for your future goals and objectives, particularly in the context of retirement planning. Whether your goal is retirement itself or other financial aspirations, such as funding education or leaving an inheritance or buying a home, I will offer practical insights for effective financial preparation. And we'll look even further into the future to address ways you can preserve your assets for the next generation.

Lastly, I've placed significant emphasis in this book on fostering a genuine understanding of the distinction between leaving an *inheritance* and leaving a *legacy*. Leaving a lasting legacy for future generations extends beyond the mere transfer of your wealth and assets and requires aligning your financial actions with your values and a broader, more meaningful purpose.

By the end of the book, you should be equipped with the knowledge you need to make informed investment decisions and navigate your financial journey successfully.

Let's get started!

CHAPTER 1

My Investing Story

I was sitting in an introductory business class at Southwest Baptist College when it happened. I was in the first row to the right of Professor William Williams (or, as we called him, Bill Bill), three chairs back. The realization struck me like a bolt of lightning—I wanted to start my own investment business. Something in the professor's lesson must have inspired me because up until then, my goal had been to pursue a calling to ministry. However, that moment of realization entirely redirected my focus. Even so, it would be years until I realized this dream.

After college, I spent a few years immersed in the world of corporate accounting, but in the aftermath of a second layoff in the agricultural industry, I found myself somewhat adrift. Instead of seeking another accounting job, I cast my net more broadly, and I began responding to every job listing

The purpose of human life is to serve and to show compassion and the will to help others.

—ALBERT SCHWEITZER

that crossed my path. Eventually, an intriguing ad caught my eye. It seemed too good to be true, but it led me into the world of institutional investing. A consulting firm hired me, and I began my career in the investment management industry, developing asset allocation strategies and investment manager research and selection for large corporate retirement plans nationwide. This marked my initiation into the institutional space, a journey that lasted until 2003.

As my career flourished in the institutional realm, circumstances led me to a moment of reflection in late 2002. Constant travel had taken its toll on my life. By that time, I had two sons, one in junior high and the other in grade school, and I was away from them frequently because of the demands of my job.

One day, I came across James Dobson's book *Bringing Up Boys*. In the book, Dobson tells the poignant story of an itinerant preacher who feels convicted about how little time he is spending with his children due to the demands of his traveling ministry.[1] He makes the decision to shift his focus from his ministry to becoming a present father. This story struck a chord. I, too, was sacrificing a lot of time with my kids due to my job. Driven by this conviction, I finally revisited the idea of starting my own investment business, and I found that technological advancements had made it more possible than ever.

I resigned from my position working with pension plans, serving clients with hundreds of millions to billions of dollars, and I ventured into a new phase of my career. March 2003 marked the approval and launch of my own firm. The transition from the institutional space to serving the affluent investor market required me to rebuild my entire career, starting afresh with a commitment to meet the unique needs of the "moms and pops" of the world.

My firm began with zero clients but eventually grew to managing over $500 million in client assets. A dream that was born in a moment of inspiration in a college classroom had finally become a thriving entrepreneurial venture, shaped by dedication, foresight, and a commitment to family values.

To be honest, although my business experienced tremendous growth, I had some early challenges to overcome. In the beginning, I underestimated the importance of meticulous planning when navigating the transition from one market to another. This oversight resulted in a slower-than-desired initial growth for the business. Furthermore, I failed to adequately anticipate the financial impact that starting a business would have on my family, given the inherent fluctuations in revenue tied not only to the assets under management but also the dynamic nature of the financial markets.

But my most consistent struggle has been figuring out how to manage our growth—both for the firm and for its human resources. I've had to learn to strike a delicate balance between client service and strategic investment in the company.

Through every struggle and every challenge of building and growing my business, I've learned that you cannot overemphasize the importance of planning and preparation! That applies to practically every human endeavor, but it's especially true when it comes to creating operating reserves (i.e., money set aside for potential future needs)—a practice we now diligently follow.

The entrepreneurial journey is unpredictable. Some days you face criticism. Other days, you receive praise and admiration. And some days, you face both. You might even get both from the same client on the same day! You have to become resilient and always prepare for the unpredictable nature of the business.

Crucially, I have leaned on the guidance of mentors, not only those within the industry but also those outside the business sphere whom I trust implicitly. These mentors have played a pivotal role in my journey, offering honest feedback that has contributed to my growth without undermining my confidence. Their input has proved invaluable in fostering personal and professional development.

Why am I sharing all of this? Because I think there is broader application to the things I've learned beyond my own entrepreneurial journey. I see the same needs in the lives of my clients as they consider their future retirement. Meticulous planning and preparedness are crucial in the face of uncertainty. Learning resilience and patience in the face of market fluctuations and life changes is incredibly important. Creating and setting aside capital reserves to meet your future needs is essential. And we all need to cultivate relationships with wise, trusted individuals (both within and outside of the professional sphere) who can contribute to our holistic personal development.

Our Evolution

The most gratifying part of my work lies in helping people find solace and contentment during pivotal life transitions. Whether it's aiding them in navigating the shift into retirement or providing support as they adjust to significant life-altering events, such as the loss of a spouse or parent, these moments are the most fulfilling. They constitute both the most challenging and the most rewarding aspects of my professional journey.

I like to think my experience in the institutional realm prepared me well to guide clients through these transitions in life. That time in my career shaped my perspective on investing, especially considering the landscape when I first entered the investment business. Back then, the individual market was a far cry from its current state, characterized by brokered transactions of individual stocks and a limited selection of mutual funds.

During that time, I learned valuable insights into genuine portfolio construction that have enabled me to help people build well-diversified portfolios. Moreover, that experience gave me a deep understanding of the diverse investment disciplines employed by different firms in managing money. For example, when a client reacts to a market fluctuation by wanting to sell all of their investments, I can help them understand the underlying investment philosophy and discipline of each of the investments and strategies in their portfolio. This is essential to sound decision-making. As Warren Buffett said, "Fear is the most contagious disease you can imagine."

One early and enduring lesson I learned during my institutional career, which remains incredibly significant today, is the critical importance of having a disciplined selling strategy in investment management. People often tend to become emotionally attached to certain investments and resist acknowledging losing ones, which can lead them to hold onto an underperforming asset for too long. Conversely, people can become attached to winners and have trouble redeploying the gains into new investments. This holds true for not only individual investors but also professional money managers.

Ensuring that each of the investment strategies that is not an index has a disciplined sell strategy is critical. Whether you handle your own investments or have a financial advisor, you need to employ this as well. Instilling a disciplined selling approach is paramount in the investment choices I make for my clients because it ensures their portfolios are continually optimized to meet their financial goals.

Interestingly, my client base has undergone a noticeable transformation over the years. It's a natural evolution that accompanies the growth of any successful firm, I suppose. In the early days, our clients mostly consisted of individuals with portfolios ranging from $100,000 to $150,000. Although we were fortunate to have a few larger clients, this was the typical scale.

My very first clients were friends from church who, despite their significant wealth, supported me as I embarked on the journey of starting my own company. To this day, they remain loyal clients, a testament to the enduring relationships forged in those initial stages.

However, as our firm has matured, so has our client profile. The asset values and income levels of our clientele experienced a substantial upswing. What once averaged $100,000 to $150,000 per client portfolio has grown tenfold, with our average client now boasting a $1 million portfolio. A shift in income dynamics also unfolded—from managing small IRAs for retirees with modest portfolios to catering to clients with significantly larger portfolios.

This evolution can be attributed to specific factors. For example, over time we began engaging with other professionals—chiefly accountants and estate planning attorneys—expanding our network and collaborating with different groups. We delved into the intricacies of total wealth management, building relationships that led to referrals and introductions to new clients. The expertise we developed in navigating complex financial situations resonated with our existing clients, who, in turn, introduced us to others.

Remarkably, we have retained many of our original clients, witnessing their financial growth alongside our own, which has been gratifying. Nothing pleases me more than to see a client reach their long-term goals and enjoy a comfortable and meaningful retirement. While we have bid farewell to a few clients over the years, our expansion into a broader market has been marked by an influx of clients with more substantial portfolios, middle-management-level incomes, and increasingly complex estates. Moreover, we have successfully tapped into a new market segment by serving institutional clients within the faith-based charity realm, carving out a niche in this sector.

This journey of growth and diversification is ultimately the result of my commitment to providing comprehensive financial solutions and adapting to the evolving needs of my clients. As I navigate these shifts, the foundational relationships endure, and my firm continues to thrive in both familiar and new markets.

I share all of this because I want you to understand the diversity of clients I've worked with over the years. I have addressed a broad range of financial circumstances, so no matter where you're starting from, there will be advice in this book to help you plan for the future.

Dealing with Today's Challenges

One of the most common challenges my clients grapple with in today's landscape mirrors a broader societal issue: the overwhelming volume of information that people are inundated with on a daily basis. The sheer magnitude of data and opinions has become a huge obstacle to clear decision-making, particularly in regard to finances. At the same time, political polarization in our country has permeated every single juncture where individuals must make decisions, greatly hindering their ability to make unbiased choices regarding investments, retirement, and various other facets of life.

The political spectrum has become a huge determining factor in financial decision-making, with those leaning toward the right often swayed by government dynamics to either shift entirely to cash or go all in on investing in things like gold and silver. Similarly, those aligning with the left experience a comparable predicament. I often find myself trying to help clients understand that businesses can thrive in diverse political environments.

Just because you may not agree with the politics of a certain business leader doesn't mean their company isn't a wise investment for getting you where you want to go. Remember, this is about your future and achieving your goals, dreams, and aspirations for yourself and your loved ones.

A secondary challenge lies in the proliferation of investment media and the plethora of financial commentators and "talking heads" providing financial advice and information. This influx of information, often conflicting or sensationalized, contributes to decision paralysis among many of my clients. They don't know whom to listen to or whom to trust.

I recall one client in particular who, despite being with us for nearly a decade, succumbed to the influence of a specific news network that shall not be named. His constant exposure to trading-focused content led him to make a series of hasty investment decisions based on short-term trends rather than long-term strategies.

In response to his frequent shifts, I implemented a safeguard that required him to document each investment decision he wanted to pursue, but it didn't change his approach. Sadly, when I analyzed his portfolio after years of this kind of short-term, media-driven decision-making, it became evident that if he had adhered to my originally outlined conservative strategy, he would have more than doubled his account value over the years.

That's just one example of the adverse impact the overconsumption of media information can make on a client's financial decisions. An abundance of news and financial content makes otherwise intelligent people feel compelled to overmanage their portfolios, and it's almost always a losing game.

Amidst this deluge, I find that our most successful clients

strike a balance—they are informed and knowledgeable without succumbing to information overload. They seek to understand, but they resist being swayed by sensationalism. They revisit their portfolio periodically, but they do not make hasty decisions or have knee-jerk reactions regarding their investments.

For those less informed, I try to provide guidance at a pace they are comfortable with. And for those clients who are susceptible to sensationalism or tempted to react impulsively to every financial headline, I constantly advocate for a more measured and strategic approach.

Another significant challenge my clients deal with these days emerges when they navigate any big, life-changing event, particularly the transition to retirement. While some people settle into retirement seamlessly, others grapple with the initial six to twelve months, especially if they formerly held executive positions. The abrupt shift to a retirement lifestyle can lead to a sense of aimlessness or emptiness. Retirees, particularly former CEOs or business owners, need some alternative focus after retirement, or they're likely to find themselves discontented, bored, or listless.

Like any good financial advisor, I strive to guide clients through this transition by emphasizing the importance of having meaningful activities post-retirement. Whether they engage in volunteering, pursuing hobbies, or finding new avenues for personal fulfillment, I always encourage them to find some purposeful endeavor to transition into. You have to plan not just for the financial aspects of retirement but also for your daily life and emotional well-being during this significant life change.

Moreover, I frequently encounter clients who, despite having the means to enjoy their wealth and retirement, hesitate to do so. They're afraid of depleting their financial resources too fast, so they avoid experiences and opportunities that could enhance their retirement years. To them, I emphasize the importance of balancing financial prudence with the enjoyment of well-deserved leisure.

Transitioning clients into retirement and ensuring they embrace a fulfilling post-career life presents a complex challenge, but it's important for people to take advantage of the opportunities their financial planning affords them. Life is unpredictable, and you never know what tomorrow holds, but if you've planned and prepared for retirement, then you deserve to enjoy whatever time you've got.

This, of course, goes beyond financial planning. It's also about having the right *mindset* and *attitude* toward retirement. When I was in college, I was pretty skeptical about the relevance of psychology, but over the years, I've come to appreciate its significance in understanding the emotional aspects of decision-making. Now, I always try to understand the mental and emotional intricacies of a client's thought processes. Understanding the emotional side of decision-making is a vital component in providing holistic financial advice and supporting clients as they navigate significant life transitions.

And that goes for you as well. As I worked on this book, I was constantly mindful of the thoughts and feelings readers would bring to the topic of retirement planning, investing, estate planning, and building a legacy. In fact, that's where we're going to start.

Before we explore investment options or the complexity of financial decisions, we're first going to help you wrap your head around these topics—retirement, investing, estate planning, legacy—so you can gain clarity and set some concrete goals for what you want to achieve.

CHAPTER 2

Setting Your Dreams and Goals

As the old saying goes, if you don't know where you're going, you're never going to get there. Imagine you set out on a road trip, but you have no destination in mind. Rather than setting a destination and mapping a route, you decide to simply drive the car until you run out of gas, and you hope that will be somewhere pleasant. Of course, the reality is there's no telling where you will eventually wind up. It could be somewhere good, or it could be somewhere awful, but you're most likely to end up in the middle of nowhere.

Unfortunately, that's how some people go through life and approach the future. They haven't thought about where they want to wind up when they reach retirement, so they aren't making plans to get there. They could be

If you want to be happy, set a goal that commands your thoughts, liberates your energy, and inspires your hopes.

—ANDREW CARNEGIE

stumbling toward catastrophe because they're simply not prepared. And that's why it's important to clarify your dreams and long-term goals before you make investing decisions. Figure out where you want to end up so you can plan the route to get there.

Similarly, some people only pursue short-term goals, or they chase after some vague idea like "making a lot of money" rather than something concrete. For example, some people invest just to beat the market or get the biggest return, but that's not really a concrete long-term goal. In fact, if that's all you're doing, you will never really reach an end goal (because you don't really have one), and you won't ultimately know when you've succeeded.

In our world, money is not an end unto itself. Money exists to meet needs, either current or future, so you have to clarify what those needs are and make plans to fulfill them. That's what should drive your goals. Otherwise, you don't know what you're shooting for, and your results could be all over the place. If you're like most people, you probably don't have the income power to keep making untargeted, scattershot investing decisions. Recently, I spoke with a gentleman who was clearly past retirement age but still working. He told me he will never be able to retire due to pouring all of his savings into a farming venture that went "belly-up."

Your goals should be tailored to meet your current and future needs. At the same time, they must be focused and achievable. If someone comes to me and says, "My goal is to beat the S&P 500 with my portfolio," then I probably won't even work with them. Why? Because that's not an achievable goal, and it isn't geared to meet their future needs. It's just a fruitless chasing after money for money's sake.

To set your goals, think carefully about what you want your money to do for you now and in the future. Typically, that future is retirement, but it can include other things. For example, it might include giving to charitable work or missions. It might include helping your kids pay for school or buy a house someday.

Whatever it is, set your goals, and then you can start making investment decisions that will move you toward meeting those goals financially.

Make Money Work for You

On one occasion, I had a woman meet with me because she was going through a divorce. She made really good money, but she had never handled the money side of things during her marriage. That had always been her husband's responsibility. Consequently, she had no idea how to plan for her future life on her own, and she found the prospect daunting.

I showed her that she had nothing to fear. We sat down together and went through her financial circumstances. We looked at her income, her savings, and her investments, and we discussed her financial goals. She told me that she wanted to be able to pay for her children's education as well as buy a house and set up retirement plans.

In a sense, she was starting over in life, but by setting those goals, we were able to put a plan together using near-term savings, intermediate savings, and long-term savings. From there, we built out her investment profile and started putting together investments that would get her to those goals in the time frame she needed. Because she set good, healthy, achievable goals and, importantly, *stuck with them*, her plan came together smoothly and made great progress over the years.

On another occasion, we had a client who became his own worst enemy. He set a fairly good goal in the beginning. In our first meeting, he identified the level of income he wanted to have during retirement, so we put together his investment portfolio with that goal in mind.

Everything was in place to get him to his financial goal by the time he retired. All he had to do was stick with the plan, maintain a long-term view, and periodically review his portfolio to make sure everything was still on track.

However, this particular client was highly susceptible to current popular investment fads. Every few months, he would come into my office and demand that we change his investment time horizon or his risk profile based on something he'd read on the internet, seen in the news, heard from an acquaintance, or happened to be feeling at the moment.

He'd say something like, "I was talking to this financial expert the other day, and he said we should be investing more in gold." Or, "I read an article online that said this one particular business is about to crash and burn because of stuff happening overseas. I want to sell all of my stock in it right now!"

Over time, against my constant advice, his changes wound up costing him a lot of money in his portfolio because he wouldn't stick with his plan. I compared his return to another client's portfolio, which was more conservative but stayed on goal. This other client's return was nearly 2 percent a year better. In real dollars, chasing fads cost my client nearly $1 million. He listened to the wrong people and chased after every whim and worry instead of identifying his goals, creating a portfolio to achieve them, and sticking with the strategy.

His story is not unique, and in fact, I shared a similar story earlier. A lot of people are susceptible to short-term, emotional thinking when it comes to their investments. I understand why this happens. When you're dealing with your money and the promise of greater wealth, it's easy to let your emotions run away with you. However, it's incredibly dangerous!

You can put together the best retirement plan in the world, but if you don't stick with it, if you listen to the wrong people and make constant changes, then even the best plan won't get you where you want to go. In the words of Warren Buffett's partner, Charlie Munger, "Waiting helps you as an investor, and a lot of people just can't stand to wait. If you didn't get the deferred-gratification gene, you've got to work very hard to overcome that."

Discovering Your Future Life

Maybe you're not sure what your long-term goals should be. Maybe you've never really thought about what you want to be working toward. If that's the case, then you probably need to sit down with a financial advisor and go through an assessment. An advisor can assess where you are today and help you figure out where you need to be when you retire. They'll help you identify any major purchases or expenses in your foreseeable future, such as buying a house or paying for college, and they will calculate how much money you're going to need to fund your retirement lifestyle.

In addition to estimating future expenses, they will help you identify your current asset level and determine the best ways for you to generate enough additional income to meet those future goals. They will also set some milestones along the way so you can track your progress. This is not a perfect science, of course. There's no one-size-fits-all solution, nor is any investment completely foolproof. However, a bit of expert guidance can greatly improve your chances of success.

Yes, you could do all of this yourself, and if that's what you decide, more power to you. It will be more time-consuming, and you may lack some expertise that will help you with your strategizing, so be sure to conduct thorough research. Even if you go it alone, you may still want to get an outside perspective on your plans at some point so that you don't accidentally overlook potential problems or defects in your plan.

It's a lot like piloting an airplane. Before you attempt to land the plane, you want to check your glide path and make sure you're lined up with the right runway. You need to make sure you're not coming in too high or too low and you don't overshoot or undershoot the runway. And of course, it's always better to seek some outside help by radioing the flight tower because they can provide you with important information to make sure you land safely. After taking everything into consideration, you may find that you need to make some adjustments while you're still in the air and have plenty of time before you finally touch down.

You don't want to be like the pilots of a commercial flight a few years ago who were heading to Branson, Missouri, but landed at Taney County Airport, Missouri, an airport with a runway nearly 50 percent shorter than Branson!

Some clients worry that they might set the wrong goals or that they might set a goal and determine down the road that they actually want to work toward something entirely different. Maybe they had some vision of their ideal retirement lifestyle, but over time, that vision has changed as their preferences and goals evolved. The good news is your goals are not static. You're not locked in forever.

For that reason, you should review your goals periodically and see if you need to adjust anything to better match your clarifying vision of a desired future. At the very least, this should happen annually or semiannually.

I had some clients who were very high earners with an incredibly high expense level. They were in their forties when they first met with me, and they didn't have any real goals for retirement. The most they could say was that they wanted to retire *someday*, but they'd never really thought about the kind of lifestyle they wanted to live or how much it would take to fund it.

When I interviewed them a bit, they determined that they simply wanted to continue to live their current lifestyle into retirement. Their expenses at that time were in the mid-six figures, which gave us a basic financial goal to work toward. They knew at least how much money they would have to be able to come up with for each year of their retirement.

With a concrete financial goal, we could begin identifying the right investments to build out a portfolio that would generate enough income by the time they reached retirement age to fund their lifestyle. The wife was surprised to discover that they didn't qualify for a certain savings account under IRS guidelines because they didn't yet have $1 million in their retirement fund. They actually had quite a bit less than they thought because they lacked financial discipline and weren't investing wisely for the future. That's common for clients with a lot of money, and that's okay.

With long-term goals in place, we were able to identify the right investments for their portfolio so they could begin generating the income they would need when they reached retirement, while still being able to live a comfortable life in the here and now.

It all starts with setting those goals. Figure out what you're working toward by envisioning your desired future lifestyle and then calculating what it's going to cost to fund it. Once you do that, then you can start to put together an investment portfolio that will achieve it in the right time frame, as long as you practice some financial discipline.

These particular clients I mentioned had been trying to generate money through investments on their own prior to working with me, but unfortunately, their previous investment strategy was largely determined by whatever the wife heard at the doctor's office, or at a conference, or while chatting with coworkers around the water cooler. In other words, she'd spent years chasing after fad investments and poorly performing short-term ideas that didn't ultimately pay off in the long run. In fact, when they first came to me, they were pretty discouraged about the potential of investing to really generate wealth, but a shift to long-term thinking put them on the right track.

You can't chase after everybody else's ideas. What other people are doing, what they're working toward, and how they plan to reach their goals may not work at all. Even if it does work for them, it may not work for you. Your needs might be different, your goals might be different, and you may not qualify for some accounts and investments they are using.

Set your own goals, and find the best way for *you* to achieve them. That's key. Don't worry about what other people are doing, and don't chase after fads and popular trends. Work with a financial advisor you trust to come up with *your own strategy*, then be disciplined about sticking to it.

HOW LONG IS RETIREMENT?

When calculating the amount of money you will need to fund your desired retirement lifestyle, bear in mind that the average length of retirement in the U.S. is about 19.5 years.[2] Plan accordingly so you don't run out of money and find yourself living solely on Social Security. Also, take into consideration that health care and medical expenses are likely to rise as you get older.

Achievable Goals

Your long-term goals can be super ambitious. There's nothing wrong with that. You can dream big about your retirement. However, those goals must also be *achievable*. The numbers have to add up. Some dreams are so ambitious that no amount of smart investing or financial discipline will ever come up with enough money to pay for it. If a fifty-year-old client comes to me with $150,000 to invest for retirement but their stated goal is to own their own private island by the time they retire, then there's probably no amount of investing that will ever get them there. It's just not an achievable goal.

To ensure your goals are achievable, you need to plan out how you're going to get from where you are now financially to where you want to go. That means figuring out your income and savings, assigning a growth rate to your current and future savings, and seeing if there's any way you can generate enough money to get there. If you need to take into account inflation and Social Security, remember that they aren't linear. Again, this is an area where a financial advisor can be beneficial because they have tools that enable you to forecast future changes.

Once you know that your goals are achievable, and you've clarified the level of growth it's going to take to meet your future income needs, then you need to come up with a game plan for generating the money. Depending on your desired future lifestyle, you may need to start saving more, become a more aggressive investor, or implement a bit more financial discipline.

You may find that getting to your goals is going to be far too difficult or require so much discipline and cost-cutting now that you're miserable, in which case, you may need to trim them back a bit. Again, all of this requires a lot of thought and careful planning, and you need to revisit and update your plans over time to make sure you stay on track.

Once you've established your goals with a sense of achievability and appropriateness, the question becomes, How should these goals dictate your investment decisions and financial strategies?

This aspect serves as the linchpin of the entire financial planning process. When your goals take precedence, they become the guiding force behind portfolio construction. The focus shifts from chasing market returns to tailoring your portfolio to serve your specific objectives.

It's important to maintain a steadfast commitment to aligning your investments with the personal aspirations of both you and your family, but a focused and committed approach will ensure a consistent trajectory along your chosen path. Unfortunately, many people fall into the trap of trying to "keep up with the Joneses." However, this mindset almost always proves futile, whether in spending or investing, because it disregards the importance of your personalized life and investment goals. It is imperative to filter out external noise and concentrate inwardly on meticulously setting *your* goals.

Once the groundwork is laid, a portfolio can be constructed that resonates with you and your loved ones. And with a well-crafted plan in place, you can navigate life's complexities with relative ease.

Remember, while money can be a powerful tool, it does not serve as a panacea for all of life's challenges. Rather, it should always be wielded as a means to an end rather than a solution in itself. Never just chase the money! Instead, use money as a tool to pursue your dreams, goals, and aspirations.

With that in mind, let's look at how you can begin investing for your future.

CHAPTER 3

Understanding Investing

There's a big difference between trading and investing, and it's important to understand the difference. If you pursue the wrong one, you're liable to derail your financial plans and fall far short of your long-term goals. So, let's clarify.

The distinction between investing and trading lies in their respective time horizons and approaches. Investing, as I see it, is firmly rooted in long-term goals and plans. It aligns with the principles discussed in the previous chapter on goal-setting and portfolio construction. It's a strategy characterized by a focus on the long haul, with adjustments made periodically to account for market and business cycles.

On the other hand, trading is marked by its short-term orientation. It can be as narrowly focused as individual

Investing should be more like watching paint dry or watching grass grow. If you want excitement, take $800 and go to Las Vegas.

—PAUL SAMUELSON

securities, sectors, or commodities, with the aim of capitalizing on fleeting market movements. This could entail day trading, which gained popularity some years back, or shorter-term trades spanning a week or a few months. Trading demands constant vigilance and active management, and it involves frequent buying and selling of narrowly defined investments. Typically, traders lack diversification, which exposes them to significant risk if they find themselves on the wrong side of a trade.

It's incredibly important to understand this distinction, especially given the proliferation of daily financial shows on television. These shows often shift their focus from broader economic and market trends to minute-by-minute updates on specific stocks or trades. This intense focus on short-term fluctuations can create a lot of confusion and noise, and if heeded, the ever-changing advice can lead to a messy portfolio, along with substantial trading costs.

Some people have success at trading, clearly. Even day traders can do well. However, successful trading requires constant attention, agility, and a high level of aggression, which makes it challenging for the average person to execute effectively. Research has shown that only about 13 percent of day traders will have consistent success over a six-month period, and only 1 percent of day traders will experience success over five years. A whopping 72 percent of day traders will end their first year with financial losses.[3] FINRA's website has a disclosure statement that offers this warning about day trading: "Day trading can be extremely risky. . . . You should be prepared to lose all of the funds that you use for day trading."[4]

Doesn't sound like a good way to build for your long-term future, does it?

In my own experience, which spans four decades, I've encountered very few professionals, let alone novices, who have excelled at trading to any significant degree. While some people may navigate these waters adeptly, the average person will struggle to achieve consistent success of any kind in the world of trading. When your goals are long-term, it's just not worth the constant headaches.

We once had a client who, intrigued by the allure of options trading, decided to delve into it with a portion of his portfolio. He attended a class held in a hotel ballroom. The instructors boasted that they would reveal all the supposed "Wall Street secrets" within a mere eight hours—a bold assertion that, in itself, proved to be far from accurate. This client, a retired gentleman with a distinguished background in government, was undoubtedly very intelligent. However, despite his acumen, he found himself ensnared in the complexities of options trading, trying to follow the spurious advice of these so-called experts.

He employed various options-trading strategies and asked us to execute these trades based on his directives. Unfortunately, he ended up losing a staggering 80 percent of his invested capital. The losses resulted from a combination of missed opportunities due to timing issues and a lack of understanding of the trades themselves.

Any time I questioned him about his trading decisions—and I frequently did—he generally cited the instructions he'd received from that class at the hotel, even though he admitted that he didn't fully comprehend the rationale behind the positions he was taking. It was a tragic situation all around. If he had taken my advice and invested for the long term, being patient and steadfast, he would have eventually generated quite a bit of money.

His experience serves as a cautionary tale that illustrates the perils of diving into unfamiliar territory without a solid understanding of the risks involved, especially when chasing after short-term investing strategies. Fortunately, he had the foresight to allocate only a portion of his wealth to these endeavors, but the losses were nonetheless substantial.

Even more tragic was the story of a minister we knew who, motivated by a desire to aid his struggling church, attended a two-day class on trading futures and options on currency. Despite our repeated warnings about the high level of risk associated with such ventures, he forged ahead, convinced that the potential rewards outweighed the dangers.

Sadly, his decision proved catastrophic. He lost his entire retirement fund trading currency futures. Again, this is a stark reminder of the volatility and complexity inherent in such markets, especially for individual traders who lack the resources and expertise of the institutional players.

As I said, in my experience, I rarely have witnessed any traders achieve sustained success in highly volatile and intricate arenas like options and currency trading. Even major financial institutions, with their vast resources and expertise, don't always emerge unscathed from such ventures. Trading, devoid of clear goals and pursued solely for profit, can lead to devastating financial consequences. I can't stress strongly enough the importance of approaching any and all investment endeavors with caution, diligence, and a thorough understanding of the associated risks. Otherwise, you are playing a dangerous game of chance with your future!

Adhere to the Strategy

The key to successful investing, in contrast to trading, lies in adhering to a well-thought-out strategy that is clearly aligned with your long-term goals. In the words of Warren Buffet, "Successful investing takes time, discipline, and patience."

Once you've established your goals, then you can begin to develop a strategy, whether independently or with the guidance of a financial advisor, and identify sound investment opportunities. These investments should be made with a long-term perspective in mind, and you should conduct periodic adjustments as economic, market, or business cycle conditions evolve, or if any particular investment causes unease.

When we help a client build an investment portfolio, we always carefully assess the economic landscape and the stage of the business cycle to determine where to allocate a client's portfolio over a span of twelve to eighteen months. We eschew short-term speculation, focusing instead on investments that align with the overarching strategy.

Whether the client decides to invest in mutual funds, exchange-traded funds (ETFs), or some alternative investment vehicle like real estate, we make sure they understand the underlying rationale behind each investment. Merely chasing the past performance of an investment without understanding the underlying factors driving it is akin to gambling. For that reason, we recommend that you delve deeper, questioning why an investment has performed well or poorly and assessing whether those conditions are likely to persist.

We hear it all the time: "This mutual fund has performed really well in the past! Surely it must be a good investment!" Although this seems to make sense, you must resist the temptation to make investment decisions based solely on past performance because past success is not necessarily indicative of future performance.

By asking probing questions and comprehensively understanding the factors driving returns for a particular investment, you can make an informed decision and avoid the pitfalls of investing solely for short-term gains.

Another kind of investing decision that you need to avoid when planning for retirement is what I like to call "water cooler" or "cocktail party" investments. This refers to an investment that everyone is buying just because they see everyone else buying it. It doesn't matter what fad investments all your friends are chasing or what amazing new investment you heard about on TV, in a commercial, or on a news program. Don't invest in something just because other people are doing it or without conducting your due diligence to understand what its future performance is likely to be and how well it fits with your overarching strategy.

And one more thing. I would never, *ever* buy an investment based on what someone told me during a seminar in a hotel ballroom.

Market Timing

Some people get obsessed with market timing when it comes to their investment decisions, but here's my advice, especially when you're investing for long-term goals: Market timing is not important, and in fact, I generally advise people to steer clear of it.

Let's clarify what we're talking about.

Market timing involves an attempt to predict when the market will rise or fall, with the strategy revolving around exiting the market before a downturn and reentering before an upswing. Typically, it's the stock market that investors try to time, though there are other markets that people play this game with.

The danger in playing games with market timing is that you can mistime your exit or your reentry. Some people get spooked by bad news and exit the market when it's still performing well because someone convinced them that a big drop was coming. Even if they manage to time their exit at the lowest point of a downturn, it's rather hard to time your reentry. If you don't get back in just before the next upswing, you could miss your opportunity and lose out on a lot of money. You might wind up sidelined while the steadfast investors reap the rewards of hanging in there.

I recall an incident from October 2023 when a client reached out to me in distress. He had just received his statement and saw that his investments were down by $8,000 for the quarter. His short-term loss made him panic, and he was convinced that he had to stop the bleeding. He told me he was contemplating pulling his money out of the market entirely and converting it into cash.

In response, I strongly advised against it. First, I reminded him that despite the recent dip, he was still showing gains for the year overall. Second, I emphasized that the market tends to experience fluctuations, and while there might be short-term setbacks, we believed that it would rebound and perform well by the year's end. In his defense, that was a volatile year. *Chart 1* (see page 28) shows the S&P 500 Index levels at each of the major headlines.[5] It was an extremely noisy year, and by the end of the third quarter, headline exhaustion made it feel as if the market was negative. However, just at the time it seemed the worst, the market went ripping up, setting seven new highs by year-end.

Thankfully, he decided to hang in there, and by the end of the year, his portfolio had experienced a remarkable upturn thanks to the stock market's almost vertical trajectory. If he had acted on his impulse to exit the market during that downturn, he would have missed out on significant returns when the market rallied strongly in the months afterward.

This anecdote serves as a reminder of the dangers of chasing after market timing. While short-term fluctuations may provoke anxiety, it's vitally important to maintain a long-term perspective

The Stories of 2023

Figure 1 | S&P 500 Index Return and Headlines in 2023

CHART 1

and resist making impulsive decisions based on fleeting market movements. Trying to time the market often leads to missed opportunities and can ultimately undermine the performance of your investments.

Market timing will transform your portfolio into one that mirrors money market returns over time, and money markets often yield as little as 2 percent or 3 percent. That's not much gain for a lot of hard work and worry. *Chart 2* (see page 29) shows the impact of being out of the market for just a few days over the last twenty years.[6] If you missed just the top twenty days, your return was basically the same as a money market account. It's just not worth the effort.

Historical data shows that the majority of stock market gains occur within a handful of days each year—around ten to fifteen

The Stories of 2023

To offer a sense of just how impressive the market return was in 2023, if you compare it against the average of all calendar year returns since the S&P 500 was incepted in 1957, it's more than double (26.3% vs. 12.1%) as shown in the **left panel** of **Figure 2**.

What we can't see in the 2023 total return figure is that the day-to-day experience for investors was more complex.

The **right panel** of **Figure 2** shows a few more statistics for the S&P 500 in 2023. Even in a big up year, there were plenty of ups and downs.

Missing out on short periods in the market, like the last nine weeks when stocks rose 16%, could have led to much lower returns (8.7% YTD as of Oct. 27 vs. 26.3% by year end) — another reminder of how trying to time the market is unlikely to leave us better off than just staying the course.

Figure 2 | S&P 500 Index by the Numbers

CHART 2

days. The catch is you can't predict which specific days they are going to be. Thus, to capture these gains, investors must remain invested throughout, rather than attempting to time the market, lest they risk missing out on significant growth and settle for marginal returns.

In the average year, the S&P 500 Index experiences a decline of 5 percent six times. Also, on average, a 10-percent decline occurs every sixteen months. A good example of this type of annual movement happened in 2023. *Chart 3* shows that there were five periods of pullback, the largest being 9.9 percent. However, 2023 ended the year up 26.3 percent, over double the average return of the S&P 500 Index from 1958 to 2023.[7]

In other words, just forget about market timing! Don't play the game. Invest for the long term and remain steadfast.

Impact of being out of the market

GTR 47

Returns of the S&P 500
Performance of a $10,000 investment between January 1, 2004 and December 29, 2023

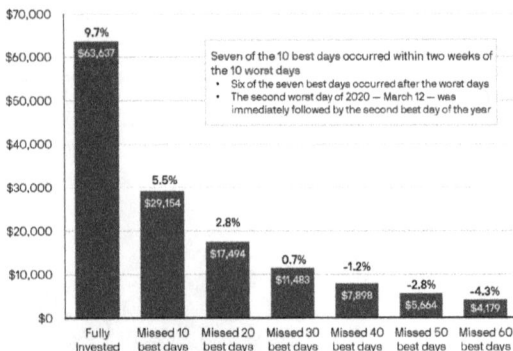

Plan to stay invested

Losses hurt more than gains feel good. Market lows can result in emotional decision making.

Taking "control" by selling out of the market after the worst days is likely to result in missing the best days that follow. Investing for the long term in a well-diversified portfolio can result in a better retirement outcome.

Seven of the 10 best days occurred within two weeks of the 10 worst days
- Six of the seven best days occurred after the worst days
- The second worst day of 2020 — March 12 — was immediately followed by the second best day of the year

Category	Value	%
Fully Invested	$63,637	9.7%
Missed 10 best days	$29,154	5.5%
Missed 20 best days	$17,494	2.8%
Missed 30 best days	$11,483	0.7%
Missed 40 best days	$7,898	-1.2%
Missed 50 best days	$5,664	-2.8%
Missed 60 best days	$4,179	-4.3%

Source: J.P. Morgan Asset Management analysis using data from Bloomberg. Returns are based on the S&P 500 Total Return Index, an unmanaged, capitalization-weighted index that measures the performance of 500 large capitalization domestic stocks representing all major industries. Indices do not include fees or operating expenses and are not available for actual investment. The hypothetical performance calculations are shown for illustrative purposes only and are not meant to be representative of actual results while investing over the time periods shown. The hypothetical performance calculations are shown gross of fees. If fees were included, returns would be lower. Hypothetical performance returns reflect the reinvestment of all dividends. The hypothetical performance results have certain inherent limitations. Unlike an actual performance record, they do not reflect actual trading, liquidity constraints, fees and other costs. Also, since the trades have not actually been executed, the results may have under- or overcompensated for the impact of certain market factors such as lack of liquidity. Simulated trading programs in general are also subject to the fact that they are designed with the benefit of hindsight. Returns will fluctuate and an investment upon redemption may be worth more or less than its original value. Past performance is not indicative of future returns. An individual cannot invest directly in an index. Data as of December 31, 2023.

J.P.Morgan
ASSET MANAGEMENT

CHART 3

Understand Your Investments

When it comes to navigating the realm of smart investing for long-term goals, my advice is straightforward: Understand what you're investing in before committing your funds. Warren Buffett often emphasizes a similar principle, urging investors to thoroughly research any potential investment opportunity. Make sure you understand the factors driving an investment's performance so you have clear expectations regarding its future prospects.

Following trends and fads can be tempting, especially when it seems like people are having some short-term success with them, but remember the timeless wisdom of Ecclesiastes 1:9: "There is nothing new under the sun." This applies to investing as well.

Furthermore, if an investment opportunity seems too good to be true, it likely is. This lesson was vividly illustrated during the market downturn of October 1987, which stemmed in large part from a flawed strategy known as "portfolio insurance." Portfolio insurance was intended to mitigate risk and limit losses by using now-primitive computer algorithms to determine the optimal allocation of assets within a portfolio. Overuse of this strategy intensified the severity of the market decline because investors using it all hedged their positions at the same time.

Despite promising to protect investors from losses during market downturns, portfolio insurance ultimately did just the opposite, intensifying a market downturn and resulting in significant losses for many people. October 19, 1987—a day that would come to be known as "Black Monday"—experienced one of the most sudden and dramatic drops in stock prices in the history of the market. So much for portfolio insurance!

The adage "If it seems too good to be true, it probably is" remains as relevant today as ever. Whether it's the dot-com bubble of the late 1990s, the real estate bubble of the mid-2000s, or the crypto craze from a few years ago, there are plenty of historical examples of failed investment fads that serve as cautionary reminders to exercise prudence and skepticism. Play the long game rather than taking a chance on the "latest and greatest" thing.

To paraphrase Warren Buffett again: The stock market is designed to transfer money from the *active* to the *patient*. So be one of the patient!

Ultimately, the key to successful investing lies in understanding the investments you choose and the reasons behind your choices. If an investment opportunity seems opaque or overly complex, it's best to steer clear and focus on investments that you can comprehend and analyze effectively. There's no one-size-fits-all approach to building a portfolio, but by adhering to sound principles and maintaining a diligent approach to research and analysis, investors can position themselves for long-term success.

I had a client come in recently who said, "I lost some money on this specific investment this year. Do I need to get out of it?"

It was a real estate investment, and that particular year was not great for real estate overall. However, it was a good relative investment that was poised to do exactly what he needed it to do over the long haul. As is so often the case, as soon as he had a disappointing year, his instinct told him to dump the investment and run. You need to fight that urge every single time it rears its head.

You have to keep thinking long-term. Look at the performance of the investment over a longer period of time. It may rise and fall in the short term, but what's the long-term performance? That is what really matters.

Active vs. Passive Investing

Finally, no discussion on investing would be complete without addressing active management vs. passive or index investing. The first index fund, the Vanguard Index Fund, was established in August 1976. Today, according to Morningstar, there are over 1,400 U.S.-based index offerings between mutual funds and ETFs.[8] Early on, the idea was to simply own the "whole" market, with a low fee, and over time you would have a nice return. It was a "set it and forget it" approach to investing.

For many years, the S&P 500 Index provided a nicely diversified portfolio by concentration and return. For example, in 1991, the top ten holdings represented 28.6 percent of the return and about 17 percent of the overall concentration. However, by the end of 2023, the top ten stocks represented 96.5 percent of the total return and 31 percent of the concentration of the index—far less diversified. Additionally, the largest exposure of the concentration is now in tech stocks.

In addition to the high concentration of a handful of stocks, the explosion of index offerings complicates the picture. Originally, indexing was focused on widely followed indexes like the S&P 500 Index, the Dow 30, the various Russell indexes, and a variety of recognized fixed income (bond) indexes. However, as the popularity of indexing grew, so did the offerings. Investment offerings expanded to include index funds based on sectors, different weightings on the popular indexes, and indexes that provided exposure to factors such as value, growth, dividends, and equal weight, just to name a few.

Many see indexing as a one-size-fits-all approach when applied against various market segments. However, not all parts of the markets are as efficient as others. Historically, the large-cap core market, as represented by the S&P 500 Index, is difficult to outperform. According to Morningstar's *US Active/Passive Barometer* report for year-end 2023, only 12.7 percent of active funds outperformed the S&P 500 Index over the last ten years.[9] But there are periods that indicate active funds do indeed offer opportunity versus the S&P. In 2022 and 2023, for example, 43 percent and 47 percent of active funds, respectively, outperformed the index.

Other segments of the markets aren't as efficient as the large-cap core segment. U.S. Small Cap Equity, International Equity, and Fixed Income markets historically have been fertile ground for active management strategies. According to the Morningstar report mentioned above, each of these market segments has proven more fertile for active strategies over long periods of time.

The strategy that I have utilized over my career, whether for my institutional consulting clients or my current clients, depends on the market segment. For U.S. Large Cap Equity exposure, I follow a core/satellite methodology, which relies on indexing the majority of the allocation to the S&P 500 Index and then supplementing it with active strategies to help focus the portfolio based on the business and economic cycles.

For the majority of the other market segments, I recommend active strategies. I find that many of the indexes that provide exposure to the U.S. Small/Mid Cap sectors, International Markets, and Fixed Income markets, in my opinion, have flaws that active managers can (and should) avoid.

Even the founder of index investing, Vanguard, offers active strategies. If they don't totally ignore active investing, then neither should you.

When to Get Rid of an Investment

There does come a time when you need to get out of a particular investment. Specifically, if it's clear that an investment isn't going to help you reach your long-term goals, then it's time to get rid of it. But don't react, or overreact, to every market adjustment. And don't let fear dictate your actions.

That applies to selling both losing *and* winning investments. Sometimes people hold onto losing investments too long because they hope to recoup their losses, but this often proves to be a fruitless endeavor. It's essential for investors to accept that it's okay to take losses and reallocate funds into potentially more lucrative opportunities.

As far as winning investments go, if a stock or investment reaches the target price that you set in your investment strategy, or if you finally reach your personal savings goal, then it's time to consider selling it and enjoying the gains. Don't keep holding on just because it might go even higher. You are aiming for your goals, not just trying to see how high a particular stock or investment might go!

Mistakes like these in investing are par for the course, whether you're a seasoned professional or a novice. That's why it's crucial to have a strict selling discipline in place. Selling can be emotionally challenging, whether it's cutting ties with winning investments even though you believe they will keep rising or holding onto losers in the hopes of breaking even. The key is not to become emotionally attached to either your winners or your losers. Your only real attachment should be to the long-term goals you're working toward.

A few years ago during a cruise, I had a conversation with a friend about his investments, and he boasted about the "amazing" profits he'd made on a Canadian stock. When I asked him at what price he sold it, he sheepishly admitted that he hadn't sold it yet, despite it being significantly off its high. I had to remind him that you only truly make money when you pocket it, not just because the stock reaches a high point. This is a common misconception, but it demonstrates the importance of being willing to sell both winners and losers when the time is right.

In essence, successful investing requires overcoming emotional biases and making rational decisions based on sound principles. Don't let fear or sentimentality cloud your judgment—be prepared to sell when necessary, whether it's to lock in gains or to cut losses. That's the key to consistent growth over the long haul!

CHAPTER 4

Building Your Portfolio

How are you going to generate the wealth that will be there to support your lifestyle or meet your long-term goals in the coming years? Chiefly, you're going to do this through an investment portfolio, which is a term that refers to a collection of assets that may include stocks, bonds, mutual funds, ETFs, real estate, and/or other forms of alternative investments.

The idea behind a portfolio is to adopt a diversified approach to managing your finances by steering clear of overconcentration in any particular asset class. In other words, you're not counting on one specific investment or type of investment to generate your wealth. You are intentionally investing a little more broadly as a strategic means of weathering economic uncertainty and achieving long-term gains.

The stock market is a device for transferring money from the impatient to the patient.

—WARREN BUFFETT

We always strongly encourage clients to align their portfolio with the goals they have established in the preceding steps, whether their goal is retirement, purchasing a car, or saving for a house. Essentially, your portfolio will serve as the implementation stage of your strategy to achieve these goals, utilizing the assets you have at hand.

As an advisor, I typically operate within a time frame spanning twelve to eighteen months for the initial allocation and structure of a client's portfolio, in conjunction with having a long-term perspective of the client's goals and risk profile.

Building a portfolio involves charting a road map toward a predetermined destination, which is generally the returns you intend to gain in the chosen time frame in order to meet your long-term goals. Once the destination is established, you can embark on constructing the portfolio, focusing on the right mix from an asset allocation perspective. To do that, you need to consider various factors such as the proportion of stocks, bonds, cash holdings, real estate, and other investment alternatives that will make up your portfolio.

Once the broad strokes of the portfolio are defined, you can shift your attention to the specifics and determine the individual building blocks of each segment. That includes things like deciding on allocations for growth and value, selecting mutual funds or other investment vehicles, identifying suitable managers, and assembling the necessary components to realize the portfolio's objectives.

Creating a portfolio should not be a haphazard process; rather, it requires diligent research and planning. It's about finding the right balance and creating exposure to different areas in alignment with your overarching goals. The overarching goal is to ensure that whatever strategy you employ maintains the desired exposure over time. Ultimately, building a portfolio is a meticulous endeavor that demands careful consideration and a focus on long-term objectives.

What Are Your Investing Options?

When considering the array of options available to investors in constructing an investment portfolio, it can feel a bit like trying to navigate a vast landscape of possibilities. From direct investments in private companies to more conventional avenues like purchasing CDs or opting for a money market account at the bank, the spectrum is wide-ranging. However, for those seeking a diversified mix tailored to their financial goals, the prevailing trend among both the general public and institutional investors is to gravitate toward diversified baskets of securities with defined objectives.

These baskets of securities, typically managed through individual accounts at asset management firms, mutual funds, or ETFs, offer investors access to specific styles and assortments of securities. Importantly, these structures provide you with access to a variety of asset classes, ranging from cash and bonds to stocks, alternative investments, and even real estate.

Let's dispel a common misconception: Being invested in a mutual fund does not mean you are solely investing in the stock market. In reality, these investment vehicles serve as delivery mechanisms for a broad array of investment strategies, each tailored to meet specific objectives—not just stocks. Mutual funds and ETFs are wrappers that investment firms use to deliver their unique or specific strategy to the mass market.

Whether through mutual funds, ETFs, or managed accounts, as an investor, you have the flexibility to access diverse investment opportunities tailored to your needs and preferences. Determining which investment options to pursue for an investment portfolio is no simple task; it requires diligent research and a thorough understanding of the available options. Initially, you need to make some fundamental decisions regarding the asset classes you wish to include in your portfolio. Whether it's large-cap stocks, small-cap stocks, mid-cap stocks, or bonds, this initial choice is going to set the stage for further exploration.

Once the asset classes are defined, you can then focus on identifying investment options within those spaces that align with your objectives. An important part of this process involves scrutinizing the underlying strategy of each investment option. Make sure that the strategy has a consistent track record of remaining within the desired asset space. For example, if you're considering a large-cap manager, you should verify that the strategy consistently adheres to large-cap investments without veering off course.

Another critical factor to consider is the track record of the investment strategy. It's almost always better to prefer strategies with a well-defined investment process that has been tested over time, as opposed to newer, untested approaches. Understanding the investment process and ensuring its repeatability are also vital considerations in the decision-making process.

Moreover, you should seek consistency in the return pattern of the investment options that you are considering. A steady and predictable return pattern is preferable to erratic fluctuations in performance. Consistency in returns, coupled with repeatability, should instill confidence in the investment strategy's ability to deliver the long-term results you're hoping for.

By meticulously evaluating these factors, you can make informed decisions when selecting investment options for your portfolio, ultimately aligning your investments with your financial goals and risk tolerance.

TYPES OF INVESTMENTS

The following is a partial list of the major kinds of investments you can include in your portfolio. They carry varying levels of risk vs. reward, so it's important to build out your portfolio carefully.

STOCKS—Stocks are portions or shares of a company. As the company generates profit, a portion is shared with stockholders through dividends. Shares can increase or decrease in value over time, so you may make more or less money than you initially paid for the stock when you decide to sell it. Stocks can be lucrative for generating long-term wealth, but there is inherent risk as well.

BONDS—Purchasing a bond means you are loaning money to whoever issued the bond (often a government, municipality, or company). When the bond reaches its maturity date, your money is returned with interest. Bonds tend to offer lower possible returns than stocks, but they are also much safer.

MUTUAL FUNDS—Mutual funds allow you to invest in a variety of securities (stocks, bonds, etc.) at the same time. While they carry some risk, they tend to be less risky than investing in individual stocks. They are usually actively managed, but not always.

EXCHANGE-TRADED FUNDS (ETFS)—Most ETFs are built similarly to mutual funds, but they are usually passively managed. They also tend to have lower entry fees than other types of funds.

ALTERNATIVE INVESTMENTS—This refers to a variety of assets whose value can grow over time, including things like real estate, gold, silver, and oil. Since alternative investments tend to behave differently than stocks and bonds, adding them to your portfolio can mitigate volatility in the market and lower the risk of your portfolio.

Avoiding Investing Mistakes

When it comes to building a portfolio, several common mistakes tend to emerge, each of which has potential consequences for investors. Among these, perhaps the most common misstep is the tendency to invest solely in the best-performing fund or stock at the time of investment.

This approach, while tempting, is fraught with risks, as performance peaks may indicate overvaluation or unsustainable growth. As an investor, you need to delve deeper and make sure you understand the real reasons for a security's performance and assess its potential for continued success.

Another common pitfall arises when individuals succumb to peer pressure or anecdotal success stories and invest in assets simply because someone else recommended them. Earlier, we called this the "water cooler" or "cocktail party" mentality. It can lead investors astray, as the recommended assets may not align with their financial objectives or risk tolerance.

Additionally, investors often fall prey to schemes that appear too good to be true, disregarding warning signs and failing to conduct due diligence. Unfortunately, these kinds of investments frequently turn out to be either disappointments or outright frauds, resulting in financial loss.

Sometimes, investors assume their portfolio is diversified simply because they hold a variety of investments. However, upon closer examination, it's revealed that these holdings have significant overlap, and they lack true diversification. For example, you might unknowingly hold too much of the same stock without realizing it. This oversight can have adverse effects on portfolio performance. This is something we see often when bringing on a new client.

Lastly, holding onto underperforming assets is a significant mistake that investors frequently make. Even when they know they should sell, many individuals hesitate, hoping to recoup their losses before taking action. This reluctance to sell can lead to prolonged periods of poor performance and potential long-term financial repercussions. To avoid this mistake, you need to exercise discipline and recognize when it's time to cut ties with an underperforming asset, regardless of any emotional attachment or a desire to break even. It is better to recognize the loss and reinvest in other opportunities that have a better potential for gain.

All of these mistakes we've just discussed are not exclusive to inexperienced investors. Even seasoned professionals can fall victim to them. Falling in love with past successes or refusing to acknowledge losses can cloud your judgment and hinder sound decision-making. Ultimately, avoiding these pitfalls requires a disciplined approach grounded in thorough research and a commitment to rational decision-making rather than emotional attachment.

A few years ago, we were using a small-cap equity manager that had an impressive long-term track record. However, over the course of several months, their performance started to underperform, and their underperformance began to accelerate. We started meeting with them frequently to make sure they were sticking to their discipline. During our third review call with the firm, it became apparent that the manager was doubling down on the type of stocks that were causing the underperformance: oil stocks. They were violating their sale discipline that they articulated when we first invested with them. After the call, we immediately sold our exposure and redeployed the funds with a new manager.

INVESTING MISTAKES TO AVOID

- Investing everything in the best-performing stock or fund at the time of investment (i.e., failing to diversify).
- Investing based on peer pressure or anecdotal success.
- Investing based on schemes that seem too good to be true.
- Assuming your portfolio is diversified without checking for overlap.
- Holding onto underperforming assets due to emotional attachment or a desire to break even.
- Holding onto winning assets even though they've hit your target price instead of selling them to enjoy the gains.

As Your Portfolio Grows

When building your investment portfolio, take the time to conduct thorough research, practice disciplined decision-making, and, as your portfolio becomes more complex, consider seeking professional guidance.

Make sure you thoroughly understand why you're investing in a particular asset and establish clear criteria for both purchasing and selling any investment. If you will maintain discipline in adhering to these criteria, it will help to mitigate any emotional decision-making, which can often lead to costly errors.

As I said, once your portfolio grows in size and complexity, involving a professional advisor will become increasingly beneficial. With a vast array of investment options available, including over 10,000 mutual funds, it's challenging for any individual investor to stay abreast of every opportunity and conduct thorough research on their own. But professional advisors have the resources and expertise to navigate this landscape effectively, which will help ensure that your investment decisions align with your goals and risk tolerance.

Furthermore, investors must not rely solely on superficial assessments of their portfolios. A portfolio may appear conservative at first glance, perhaps due to its predominant allocation to bonds. However, a deeper analysis may reveal that these bonds possess aggressive characteristics, such as long maturities and lower quality ratings. In unfavorable market conditions, these bonds may underperform significantly, contradicting the portfolio's perceived conservative nature.

Scrutinize Your Portfolio

Ultimately, as an investor, you must lift the hood, so to speak, and scrutinize your portfolio's underlying investments to truly understand their risk profile and potential performance. Remember, the labels attached to investment vehicles, such as bond funds or stocks, do not necessarily dictate their risk levels. By delving deeper into your portfolio and seeking professional guidance when necessary, you will be able to make informed decisions and avoid costly mistakes in building your investment portfolio.

Another important discipline to uphold when constructing your investment portfolio is the practice of *rebalancing*. Over time, some of your investments may perform better than others, depending on market fluctuations, which could cause your portfolio's asset allocation to shift away from your target. When that happens, you can proactively adjust, or rebalance, your portfolio by selling assets that have performed well and reinvesting the proceeds into assets that have underperformed. By doing so, you ensure that your portfolio remains aligned with your long-term investment objectives and risk tolerance.

To that end, regular reviews of each investment within the portfolio are essential. You should assess whether these investments still fulfill their intended purpose and remain suitable given the prevailing market and business conditions. How often should you review your investments? At a bare minimum, I recommend conducting an annual review of your portfolio and assessing whether or not you need to rebalance your investments.

It's also a good idea to review your portfolio anytime you go through a significant life change that might cause changes in your long-term goals or life circumstances. Life events that warrant a portfolio review may include marriage, divorce, the birth of a child, or a career change.

Additionally, you may want to review your portfolio during significant market fluctuations. However, you must resist the urge to react to short-term market fluctuations with knee-jerk decision-making. Remember, reviewing your portfolio is not about reacting to the short term but ensuring your portfolio is still aligned with your long-term goals. It is also about understanding long-term performance and how your portfolio is positioned for the broader business cycles and economic trends.

By staying attuned to these factors, you can make informed decisions about the composition of your portfolio, positioning yourself for long-term success while minimizing unnecessary risks.

CHAPTER 5

Estate Planning

W e've talked a lot about generating wealth so that you can achieve your long-term goals and live your desired lifestyle during retirement. But what's going to happen to all of the wealth and assets you've acquired during your lifetime when you finally leave it all behind? If you don't have a good estate plan, then they may not be preserved or distributed in the ways you want.

Estate planning is all about ensuring that when you pass on or if you become incapacitated for some reason, your wealth and assets will be distributed according to your wishes rather than being subject to the dictates of the state or other external entities. However, getting it right requires thoughtful consideration and strategic decision-making to ensure that your legacy is preserved and transferred in alignment with your intentions.

Estate planning is an important and everlasting gift you can give your family.

—SUZE ORMAN

Getting It Wrong

The importance of estate planning cannot be overstated, as demonstrated by a recent scenario we encountered. We have a client who runs a charity, and they received an inheritance from an individual who had an estate plan in place. However, rather than seeking legal counsel from an attorney experienced in estate planning, the benefactor had consulted a friend who was a minister to assist with the estate plan. Unfortunately, this decision resulted in a chaotic and complicated situation.

The assets within the estate were not properly titled, and there were errors in naming beneficiaries. In one instance, the minister misidentified a beneficiary to several mutual fund companies where the assets were held. Consequently, our client had to navigate legal proceedings, including appearing before a judge in probate court to verify the correct beneficiaries without going to trial.

Furthermore, due to the complex structure of the estate, we and another firm were required to open accounts at numerous financial institutions to facilitate the transfer of assets to the designated charities. The legal fees incurred by the estate to rectify these errors far exceeded what would have been spent on establishing a proper trust during the individual's lifetime. This process has taken over three years to complete, costing several thousands of dollars in attorney fees, probate costs, and other professional fees.

This situation underscores the challenges and complications that arise when estate planning is not conducted appropriately. Without a solid estate plan, heirs may encounter difficulties accessing the intended funds, leading to delays and potential disputes. However, estate planning doesn't necessarily have to be intricate. Simple strategies, such as beneficiary designations or trusts outlined in wills, can effectively transfer assets according to one's wishes.

WHAT IS PROBATE COURT?

Probate court is a specialized court that deals with the legal process of administering the estate of someone who has passed away, which typically entails the distribution of assets according to either a will or state law, as well as handling any outstanding debts. The goal of probate court is to ensure that the deceased person's wishes are carried out, that any outstanding debts or taxes are paid, and that disputes and disagreements among beneficiaries are resolved. Rules governing probate court vary from state to state, but in general, the probate process can take six to twelve months.

Getting It Right

Ultimately, the complexity of your estate plan should be tailored to your circumstances, so seeking guidance from a knowledgeable attorney is important. Unfortunately, some people have outdated estate plans that are unnecessarily convoluted due to incremental additions over time. For that reason, we recommend periodic reviews and updates to ensure that your estate plan remains effective and reflective of your current intentions and is current with estate tax law.

A couple of years ago, we had a client whose attorney was constantly amending their estate documents, almost once or twice a year. Despite the estate not being overly complex, the documents ended up spanning a couple of hundred pages. Recognizing the need for a more streamlined approach, we suggested bringing in a different attorney to review the situation.

After this review, we were able to simplify the estate documents down to a concise fifteen pages. This restructuring not only cleaned up the documents but also made future administration much more manageable.

Estate planning can range from simple to complex, regardless of the size of the estate. It's not the magnitude of the assets that determines the complexity, but rather the unique circumstances of the estate. Keep that in mind, and make sure you work with an attorney who won't introduce unnecessary complexity.

Everyone should have some form of estate plan in place, whether it involves straightforward beneficiary designations for accounts or a more elaborate arrangement such as a will and trust, especially individuals with businesses or complex assets. Additionally, considerations must be made for minor children or heirs with disabilities.

We frequently encounter challenges related to minor children in estate planning. Determining guardianship for minor children is a critical decision, yet it often becomes a major hurdle for families. Some individuals may procrastinate addressing this issue, causing delays in completing their estate plan.

In our experience, we advise young families in particular to prioritize addressing guardianship for minor children as the first step in their estate planning process. By tackling this important decision early on, families can streamline the rest of the planning process and avoid potential complications in the future.

Failing to address these factors could have severe consequences, particularly in the case of children with disabilities, where improper estate planning could jeopardize their eligibility for government aid based on how assets are distributed.

But an estate plan is about more than ensuring children will be taken care of or that your assets will be distributed according to your needs. It's also about mitigating the burden of estate taxes. If you have a lot of wealth, there's a good chance the federal government is going to take a big bite out of it. In fact, federal estate taxes can range from 18 percent to 40 percent, depending on how much you leave behind. Some states levy estate taxes as well. The more affluent you are, the bigger a concern this should be. Your estate plan can potentially reduce the tax burden through tax-free lifetime gifts, charitable contributions, gifts to irrevocable trusts, and other strategies.

Currently estates with the value of $12.92 million or less for individuals and $25.84 million or less for married couples pass tax-free at the federal level. However, this exemption sunsets on December 31, 2025. Therefore, it is important to make sure your estate documents are reviewed and account for this change if Congress does not address this.

At the time of this writing, the states that charge estate taxes are Connecticut, Hawaii, Illinois, Maine, Maryland, Massachusetts, Minnesota, New York, Oregon, Rhode Island, Vermont, and Washington, in addition to the District of Columbia.

Indeed, estate planning is a multifaceted process that requires careful consideration of various factors. It's essential to approach it with diligence and seek professional guidance to ensure that your wishes are properly documented and your loved ones are adequately provided for in the event of your passing.

The most important thing you can do, in my view, is to enlist the services of a skilled estate planning attorney who can craft a comprehensive plan tailored to your needs. While a general attorney may suffice for simpler estates, it's far better to seek out an estate planning attorney, especially for more complex situations. We've encountered instances where generalist attorneys have drafted flawed documents, such as mislabeling a revocable trust as irrevocable, leading to unnecessary complications.

Finding the right estate planning attorney is also incredibly important, much like selecting any professional advisor or service provider. Personal referrals often prove to be the most reliable method for identifying reputable professionals in this field. You need to work with someone with whom you can establish a level of comfort and trust, so take the time to research and engage with an attorney who understands your circumstances and can guide you through the estate planning process effectively.

In some cases, particularly with intricate estates, involving your accountant and financial advisor may be necessary to ensure all aspects are properly addressed. As we will discuss further in the next chapter, building the right team of professionals will ensure that your estate plan is thorough and accurately reflects your wishes and objectives.

Will vs. Trust

Of course, the biggest mistake you can make with estate planning—a mistake that is very common—is to simply have no plan in place at all. It is shocking how many people, even people with a lot of wealth and assets, never take the time to create an estate plan and just leave a big mess behind them when they pass on. That mess has to be dealt with by loved ones, who wind up going through probate and possibly bickering over distribution. The fallout can be profoundly detrimental to the family.

Some people don't have an estate plan because they assume that their will provides comprehensive coverage. Those individuals, unfortunately, misunderstand the purpose and power of a will. They think a will is going to safeguard their assets and dictate their distribution, but that is not actually the purpose or the power of a will. A will merely outlines your wishes to the court so that the court can make reasonable decisions about what to do with your assets. It does not, however, circumvent the probate process. Relying solely on a will typically results in a lengthy and cumbersome probate process, as assets are subject to court oversight and distribution.

To prevent that, you need to create a trust. A trust is essentially an arrangement that allows an appointed trustee to hold your assets on behalf of your beneficiaries, and unlike a will, a trust combined with proper titling documents can indeed help avoid probate altogether.

Choosing the right trustee is incredibly important, so make sure it's someone you trust to safeguard your assets, carry out your wishes (even if that requires difficult decisions), and accept the responsibility.

WHAT IS A TRUST?

A trust is a legal arrangement in which your assets are transferred to a trustee who manages them for the benefit of your beneficiaries. Your trustee follows the instructions that you provide in the trust agreement when it comes to managing your assets and distributing them to beneficiaries. The benefits of such an arrangement include avoiding probate, protecting your assets, and ensuring that your wishes are carried out once you're gone.

As I mentioned earlier, some people establish a trust but then they forget to transfer their assets into it. As a result, even with a trust in place, their assets remain outside its purview, rendering the trust ineffective. An example shared by a client highlights this oversight. Despite having a trust prepared, this particular client failed to transfer any assets into it, essentially rendering the trust moot. If we had not rectified the situation, their intended beneficiaries and heirs would have had a mess on their hands when that person passed away.

Let me say it again: It is important for you to not only create a trust but also ensure that your assets are properly titled within it. An estate planning attorney can help you with this. Don't put it off any longer! It's too important.

CHAPTER 6

Building Your Team

I f you want to get your finances in order, then it's important to establish the right financial team at the outset. The easiest way to put together a team of experts to handle all aspects of your financial plans is to approach a so-called "one-stop shop," but we do not recommend this approach. In fact, I personally strongly discourage it. In my experience, one-stop shops often fail to meet expectations in one or several key areas of financial planning.

These establishments offer a wide array of services, encompassing financial advice, product offerings (insurance, annuities, etc.), legal guidance, and accounting, all within a single entity. While this setup may appear convenient, it can lead to problems, as we've witnessed time and time again. We've worked with many clients who left such firms in search of more personalized assistance.

Teamwork is the secret that makes common people achieve uncommon results.

—IFEANYI ENOCH ONUOHA

The drawback of one-stop shops lies chiefly in their tendency to prioritize self-interest. And because they are providing a wide array of services, if any aspect of their services falters, it could necessitate a complete overhaul of the relationship, resulting in unnecessary disruptions. Moreover, we've heard of certain firms designating themselves as trustees for clients' trusts without the clients' full comprehension, resulting in complications down the road.

Also, the prevailing trend of one-stop shops overlooks the significance of diverse perspectives in financial planning. Conversely, engaging specialists who are independent of each other allows you to access a spectrum of ideas and strategies. For example, we recently collaborated with an elder law attorney on behalf of a client facing potential dementia. While the initial estate plan focused on navigating Medicaid intricacies, we advocated for a simpler approach considering the client's age and asset portfolio.

Independent experts can offer unique insights, opposing points of view, and even outside accountability. In our practice, we frequently collaborate closely with attorneys and accountants who are independent of our business, and we each contribute our own unique expertise and viewpoints. This cooperative yet independent approach enables us to craft tailored solutions that align with our clients' needs, a level of customization often absent in one-stop shops.

Ultimately, assembling a diversified team of professionals ensures a more holistic and effective financial plan.

Who Belongs on Your Team?

When it comes to assembling your financial team, you need to consider carefully who else should be involved. Who are the star players on this winning team going to be?

The first people you may want to consider are your own children. Should the next generation be involved in your financial plans? In my experience, this can certainly be beneficial and make the eventual transition easier. However, it may also present challenges in certain family dynamics. We've seen a few rare occasions where the involvement of children was a problem because of conflicting interests and complex family dynamics.

We've also seen a general trend where the more wealth a person has, the more problematic family relationship dynamics can be. However, even then, it's worth at least considering getting the children involved.

Beyond your own family, there are three main independent players who need to be on your team, and as long as you've got these three players, then you will have a well-rounded team that's going to look out for your best interests. Their independence from one another is key to ensuring that your interests are safeguarded.

Who are these three players?

1. **A FINANCIAL PLANNER/ADVISOR**

2. **AN ESTATE PLANNING ATTORNEY**

3. **AN ACCOUNTANT**

FINANCIAL PLANNER/ADVISOR—A financial planner helps clients manage their money, set financial goals, and create strategies for achieving those goals. They provide advice and ongoing support on many aspects of personal finance, including saving, investing, retirement planning, and estate planning.

ESTATE PLANNING ATTORNEY—An estate planning attorney is a licensed attorney who helps clients plan for the distribution of their wealth and assets after they pass away or become incapacitated. This often includes drafting a will, setting up a trust, designating beneficiaries, and creating a power of attorney document.

ACCOUNTANT—The primary role of an accountant is to help clients manage their finances effectively, which may include setting a budget, developing a financial plan, optimizing their tax situation, and managing debt. They can also provide advice about legal aspects of investing, retirement planning, and estate planning.

We have an older client who is very affluent, and their financial and family situation is very complex. We maintain a close relationship with her accountant, even though the accountant works independently from us. Together, we keep a watchful eye on her financial affairs, ensuring that her decisions are autonomous and sound.

By having an independent team in place, we not only mitigate the risk of potential elder abuse, but we can also detect and address any concerns promptly. This approach allows us to act swiftly should we suspect any undue influence, whether from family members or external parties. Ultimately, having a collaborative yet independent team ensures that your financial well-being remains a top priority, free from outside interference.

Getting the Right Team Members

What if you work hard to put together an independent team, but over time, you begin to feel like one of your team members isn't really fulfilling their role effectively? This does happen sometimes, though if you do your research up front and get referrals from trustworthy people, then it is far less likely.

If you feel like a member of your financial team isn't fulfilling their role effectively, my advice is to address the issue head-on. We've encountered situations where clients have expressed concerns about certain professionals on their team, and our approach is always to take prompt action.

For example, we had a client with an attorney who seemed to be overstepping their role as trustee, unnecessarily complicating the estate documents. Both myself and the client's accountant shared our reservations about this attorney's approach directly to the attorney. Ultimately, the problem was resolved, and the client was pleased with the outcome. However, if we hadn't addressed the problem promptly, it could have caused the client or their eventual heirs a lot of problems.

If there's a problem with a member of your financial team, don't wait. Deal with problems and poor performance early and directly. First, if you're unsure about a team member's performance or decisions they've made on your behalf, I recommend seeking a second opinion. Before we confronted our client's attorney, we consulted two other attorneys who confirmed our suspicions about the outdated and convoluted nature of the documents.

Similarly, we've encountered instances where clients were overpaying taxes due to their accountant's advice. Upon our recommendation, they sought opinions from different accountants, which led to significant tax savings.

By being proactive and seeking input from other trusted professionals, you can ensure you're receiving the best possible advice and service. Ultimately, fostering open communication and collaboration within your financial planning team is key to addressing any concerns and optimizing your outcomes.

Where to Look

At this point, you might wonder where you're supposed to find these amazing, independent, trustworthy team members. You could simply choose an accountant, financial planner, and attorney at random off a Google search. I don't recommend that. Your financial plans are too important to leave to chance.

If you already have one or two team members, ask them for referrals. Since you already trust your current team members, you can probably trust their recommendation better than strangers on the internet or chance. Our clients always ask us for referrals, and we're happy to give them.

But what if you ask your current team members for a referral, and they can't give you one? For example, what if you ask your estate planning attorney to recommend an accountant, and he says, "I don't really know any good accountants. Sorry." In my opinion, that's a bit problematic. At the very least, it means they need to develop better communication with competent people in related industries around them.

Of course, you can also ask trusted family members or friends, especially people you know who are in a similar financial situation as you. This can be as simple as asking, "Who are you using as an accountant? Are they doing a good job? I'm looking for a good attorney to help with my financial plans."

Ultimately, whom you choose to include on your financial planning team is incredibly important, so you want to make sure you get it right. Reliable, experienced, and independent team members are more likely to help you make smart financial decisions that will guard against complications and problems down the road so you can meet your goals with confidence.

CHAPTER 7

Plan and Preserve a Legacy

I n all of your financial, retirement, and estate planning, there is something more important than money and assets that must be woven into every decision you make and every goal you set. What is that one thing? Your legacy.

Recently I was reviewing some of my notes from a conference and came across a quote from the keynote speaker, John Maxwell. As an aside, he is one of my favorite authors and speakers, and I highly recommend his books. John stated the following:

> "An inheritance is what you leave to people; a legacy is what you leave in people."

You need to be planning for more than just the eventual transfer of your

Carve your name on hearts, not gravestones. A legacy is written into the minds of others and the tales they share about you.

—SHANNON L. ALDER

wealth and assets to the next generation. You also need to be thinking very carefully, and strategically, about the values and mission you are going to perpetuate into the future. Your impact on your family, your community, and the world doesn't have to end when you pass on.

Legacy planning ensures that beyond the distribution of assets, your principles and beliefs will be carried forward. For example, we have a client who is deeply invested in charitable work, with specific values he wishes to uphold even after his passing. However, when he came to us, he made it clear that he harbored doubts about whether his children would continue supporting these causes. To safeguard his philanthropic legacy, he designated a separate trustee to oversee these endeavors, which ensured that his values would endure globally, not just locally.

Preserving What Matters to You

In essence, legacy planning is about preserving and promoting what matters most to you and the ways in which you hope to leave a lasting impact on future generations. It's a means of ensuring that your life's work and values continue to shape the world, even in your absence.

In my own life, there are certain negative legacies that I haven't wanted to perpetuate within my family, and others that I am determined to pass on through my way of life. Chiefly, I have wanted to impart the legacy of family, something I sorely missed growing up in a broken home.

To that end, I have worked hard to emphasize the importance of family bonds, staying committed to one's spouse, and prioritizing the well-being of our children. Years ago, as I reflected on my life (which I spoke about a bit in the first chapter), I realized that if I continued in my demanding job, I wouldn't be able to fully invest in my children or prioritize my marriage. My actions wouldn't align with my legacy goals. A career change was in order.

The second legacy I seek to instill is my faith and its profound importance in life. Despite my father's active involvement in church, his subsequent abandonment of my family left a bitter taste. While I could have let his actions tarnish my perception of God, I made a conscious decision not to allow human failings to influence my own faith.

It was important for me to convey to my children that people may disappoint them, but their faith in God should remain steadfast and unwavering. Even people who are of the faith or claim to have a relationship with God are going to let my children down or contradict their purported faith by their actions. In my own life, my father was the clearest example of this, but the hypocrisy of his actions didn't have to rob me of my faith.

The message I wanted to instill in my children is this: Never let someone else's choices impact your relationship with God or your view of God. It's something I had to learn in my own life, and I want to pass it on to my children. I have a quote from my former pastor Max Morris in the front of one of my Bibles that served as a sort of "North Star" for me in my spiritual journey: "If a hypocrite stands between you and God, they are closer to God than you are."

The third legacy I want to pass on is stewardship—the faithful use of our resources—and I mean far more than just financial stewardship. For me, stewardship includes your time, talent, and treasure. It's something I first learned when I was young, and it's a lesson I have passed along to my children and others whom I have had the opportunity to teach. My wife and I spent nine years teaching sixth-grade kids at church, and we taught this concept of stewardship to them and then provided opportunities for them to spend time serving others. It was always one of the highlights of the year.

Many times, my children have seen me serve others with my time, talent, and treasure in a lot of different capacities because I think it's important that they see it from me and not just hear it. They've seen the way I act according to my values, and as a result, I believe it is more likely that they will perpetuate this legacy to future generations.

Finding Your Legacy

What legacy do you want to pass along to your heirs and beneficiaries? What are the values and mission you want them to perpetuate? What impact do you hope to continue to make even long after you're gone? For some people, answering these questions is easy because they've already thought about them for a long time.

However, other people might not have pinpointed exactly what they want their legacy to encompass. That's okay. If you haven't clarified the values and mission you hope to perpetuate after you're gone, my advice would be to take a step back and reflect on what truly motivates you. Spend some time in introspection.

Ask yourself, "What gives me purpose? What compels me to get out of bed every morning?" These are questions only you can answer, and we all have different drives and passions. I have a son who is not inherently driven to pursue entrepreneurship like me. That's not going to be something he embraces, nor will it be his legacy to his own children, because that's not what truly matters to him. And there's nothing wrong with that. He will have to decide for himself what values and mission he hopes to perpetuate in the future.

If you're unable to figure out what truly gives you purpose and motivates you, then it might be difficult to figure out what you want your legacy to be. In that case, maybe you need to think a bit more simply. How do you want other people to remember you? That's a simpler way to consider your legacy. If you can figure out how you want to be remembered, you can begin to consider what you need to do in order to shape and influence the memory of you.

Everyone Leaves a Legacy

Here's the thing: Everyone leaves a legacy, whether they consciously plan it or not. I once had a client whose father defied the odds and lived to be one hundred years old, proudly declaring, "I beat the actuaries again," referring to his pension at each of our quarterly meetings. Despite his advanced age, when his wife fell ill, he showed unwavering devotion by visiting her in the nursing home every day.

Even in his eighties and early nineties, he packed his lunch and made the trip, sacrificing his own well-being for hers. Witnessing this commitment deeply impacted me, and I shared with his son how his father exemplified what it truly means to honor marriage vows, especially during challenging times. This was his legacy he left to me.

Another client, who happened to be the father-in-law of the first client I just talked about, left a different kind of legacy—one of generosity. Each Christmas, he orchestrated a meaningful tradition where we all gathered for breakfast or sometimes lunch. Each participant was required to carry a $100 bill in their pocket. We dispersed throughout the city, seeking out individuals to whom we felt compelled to give this gift, believing it to be a prompting from God.

Afterward, we reconvened and shared our experiences as a small group. This practice, guided by the father-in-law, taught me the importance of being prepared to bless others unexpectedly. I've passed this valuable lesson on to my children, ensuring that the legacy of generosity continues to flourish.

My children have learned from my example that giving is a fundamental part of our family ethos. They often approach me to ask for one of the $50 bills I carry in my wallet for the purpose of assisting someone in need. Even my wife, who has historically been more reserved and cautious with money, has embraced this spirit of generosity. She now actively seeks opportunities to give, even suggesting financial support for friends going through hardships.

This legacy of generosity, which was passed down to me, is one I've been eager to impart to my family. While I've always been inclined to give, that client's father-in-law taught me the importance of a generosity that transcends mere tax benefits. It's about giving without expecting any recognition or financial gain. I strive to practice this kind of giving discreetly, ensuring that the focus remains on the act itself rather than on any personal gain.

For me, leaving a legacy means instilling in my children values that extend beyond material wealth. I want them to remember me as someone who prioritized family, love, and compassion above all else. Money may come and go, but the lessons of kindness and love endure for generations.

My friend Bill High has invested significant time and research into this, as he helps families in this area. He encourages us to remember this: "The great legacies are not those that we merely leave behind, but they are living legacies—it is what we instill in people that lives beyond our lifetime."

ON LEGACY

From preachers to actors to authors to athletes, many people have thought about and talked about the kind of legacy they want to leave behind. Consider the following quotes.

GEORGE FOREMAN—"I say to my kids . . . you're not going to be the biggest, fastest, prettiest, the best athlete, but you can be the nicest person that anyone has ever met in their life. And I want to leave the legacy that being kind is a true treasure."

MARK BATTERSON—"You'll never be the ideal parent, but you can be a parent who prays. Prayer is your highest honor as a parent. Prayer turns regular parents into prophets who change the destinies of their children, grandchildren, and every future generation. The prayers you pray for your children are the greatest legacy you can leave."

OG MANDINO—"The greatest legacy we can leave our children is happy memories."

KEVIN DEYOUNG—"The best way to leave a legacy is to believe, teach, defend, and promote what is true."

JAMES DOBSON—"There is nothing more important than parents passing on a generational legacy of faith and values to their children."

Communicating Your Values

What family legacy are you passing along to the next generation? If there are values or a family mission that you hope to perpetuate, then you need to be intentionally communicating them and modeling those values. Engage in open discussions about why certain values are important and how they drive your actions.

I've found that both modeling behaviors *and* actively teaching my children through dialogue are effective methods. It's unrealistic to expect that values will be understood without discussion or demonstration.

Of course, the gentleman who cared for his wife by visiting her every day didn't necessarily talk about his actions, but his commitment to her spoke volumes. On the other hand, the other gentleman openly discussed the joy he found in giving without expecting recognition. His willingness to share his motivations inspired me to explore the deeper significance of generosity.

In my own journey, I've tried to convey to my children why certain values matter and why I want to pass them on as part of our family legacy. Whether through conversation or shared experiences, I have constantly looked for ways to articulate the reasons behind our actions and the values we hold dear.

The experiences I had growing up, particularly with my parents, deeply influenced the way I raised my own children. My boys are well aware of the pain I went through when my father left and how my relationship with my mother evolved and got stronger afterward. It was after my father's departure that I truly bonded with my mother and became very close to her.

From this, my boys witnessed the importance of commitment and respect in a marriage. Even when my wife and I experienced disagreements or challenges, our children understood that disrespecting their mother was never acceptable. This principle remains true today, even with my grandsons, who are now witnessing the same respect and love for their "Gigi."

I believe these values are absolutely vital, yet they are often overlooked in today's society. In a world where visual learning dominates, certain intangible values, like respect and commitment, are sometimes sidelined. It's a trend I find concerning, as these values are foundational to healthy relationships and families. I've tried to embody them in my own life, and it is my hope that my children and grandchildren will continue to embody them.

What about you? What are the values that matter most to you, and what are you doing to ensure that the next generation will embrace them? Have you discussed them? Have you embodied them in the choices you've made? If not, it may be time for an honest self-assessment and some profound life changes.

It's Never Too Late

Sadly, there are instances I've seen where clients lack any sort of positive legacy or fail to share one with the next generation. For instance, I have a client who achieved great financial success but now regrets not instilling the right values in his children. He acknowledges that while he will leave them with considerable wealth, their lives are far from fulfilled or meaningful. This unfortunate scenario is far more common than you might think.

On a brighter note, another individual I work with has set a positive example for his children. He prioritized his marriage and family, participated in charitable work, and practiced his faith, while also excelling in his career. His children observed and absorbed these values, and they have gone on to mirror his dedication to family, faith, and community involvement. They've embraced similar paths, establishing loving marriages, starting families, and remaining active in their faith.

The fact is children often follow in our footsteps, whether positively or negatively, because they are shaped and influenced by our actions. It's not enough to talk the talk. You have to live your values. But in order to do that, you first have to consciously decide what legacy you want to leave, for your family and thereby for the world.

I believe that if we leave the right legacy for our children, it will naturally extend to others we encounter in life. Conversely, if we focus solely on external perceptions at the expense of family, both legacies will suffer.

Reflecting on a former boss's funeral, I realized the importance of leaving behind a legacy that resonates with those closest to us. Hearing praises for someone I hardly knew made me vow to ensure my own legacy aligns with who I truly am.

Maybe you've found all of this talk about leaving a legacy discouraging because you feel like you've wasted so many years *not* intentionally building a legacy for your family. Maybe you think it's too late. Allow me to set your mind at ease. I believe it's never too late to start building a lasting legacy of values and mission as long as you're still alive.

And if you've made mistakes in the past, simply acknowledge them honestly and start taking steps to rectify your life. This honest redirection can make a powerful impact on your family, and help you lay the foundation for a positive legacy moving forward, no matter how "late in the game" it may seem.

Ready for the Future

I never really set out to write a book. It was just not a personal goal of mine. As I mentioned earlier, it was a trusted friend who said, with a twinkle in his eye, "You need to write a book." That simple suggestion became a call to action driven by a deep understanding of the challenges my clients face in the world of investments. My friend saw something in me—a wealth of experience, a unique perspective—that he believed could benefit a wider audience.

I truly hope you feel my effort was worthwhile. Yes, I could have simply continued serving my clients in my usual capacity, but I have an unwavering desire to help as many people as possible. Every day, I work closely with people from many different walks of life, guiding them through the labyrinth of financial decisions. This book is an extension of that mission. I want readers to grasp the essence of successful retirement planning, regardless of where they stand on the investment spectrum or what dreams they harbor for their future. After all, retirement isn't just a phase; it's a strategic endeavor requiring personalized attention.

In the preceding chapters, I have tried to reveal the various pieces that make up good financial planning. We talked about the importance of setting your own long-term goals so you know what you're working toward. Then we discussed what it means to create a well-rounded investment portfolio, distinguishing timeless strategies from fleeting temptations, so you can make progress toward your goals.

I encourage you to avoid alarmist media reports, "water cooler" investment talk, or just doing what everyone else is doing. Your portfolio is about achieving your own goals, not anyone else's. To that end, we looked at some of the different kinds of investments you can use to diversify your portfolio based on your own goals and risk profile.

Then we looked at the importance of estate planning for protecting your wealth and assets and preserving them for future generations. Remember, a will does not guarantee that your assets will be distributed according to your wishes. It's designed only to provide some guidance for probate court. If you really want to be sure that your wishes will be carried out, then you need to create a trust, place your assets in that trust, and appoint a trustee to oversee it.

We also talked about putting together a financial team of experienced experts who can work together to ensure every aspect of your financial future is addressed. I recommended that you include a financial planner, an estate planning attorney, and an accountant on that team, but avoid one-stop shops. If your team members are independent of each other, then they will bring more diverse perspectives and a greater sense of accountability. To find the best people, get referrals from those you trust: friends, family, colleagues, or current financial team members.

You also might consider getting your children involved in your financial planning, since they are the ones who will have to deal with the estate someday. However, family dynamics may make this problematic.

Finally, we explored the heartbeat of it all: your legacy. As we said, planning for the future is about more than passing down assets; it's also about imbuing your financial choices with purpose, ensuring that you make a lasting impact on generations to come through your own vision and mission. If you've never really clarified your legacy, think about what matters most to you and how you want people to remember you.

You should now have a good idea of the next steps you need to take to begin shaping your financial future, preserving your wealth and assets, achieving your long-term retirement goals, and building a legacy that will endure long after you're gone. I've tried to keep this book straightforward and easy to read to protect you from information overload.

Remember, a lot of bad advice is out there, particularly in regard to investments. From seminars in hotel ballrooms to alarmist media personalities, a lot of people will try to push and pull you in various directions. Even if you start off on the right foot, you can easily get derailed if you don't resist making knee-jerk, emotional decisions. Stay focused on your long-term goals, especially the retirement lifestyle you hope to live, and resist the temptation to chase after quick gains and fleeting trends.

With all of that in mind, you're ready to start setting goals and building toward your future. The first step is to assess your current financial situation so that you know what you have to work with. As you bring all the pieces together, you might find that you have more to work with than you realized. After that, you can set your goals and clarify the retirement lifestyle you hope to achieve someday. From there, you can begin charting your course, building your investment portfolio, and putting together your financial team.

If you have any further questions, you can always reach out to me. Email me, call me, write me a handwritten letter—whatever you prefer. Just remember, this is about *your* dreams, *your* goals, and *your* legacy, so dare to dream big and aim high!

CHECKLIST FOR
RETIREMENT PLANNING

1. Conduct an assessment of your current financial situation to get a big-picture view of how much you have to work with.

2. Determine what your long-term financial goals are.
   a. What sort of lifestyle do you hope to enjoy during retirement? How much annual income will you need to fund it?
   b. Are there any large-scale purchases that you want to fund in the future (a child's education, buying a home, etc.)?

3. Figure out how much money you're going to need to generate between now and then to meet those goals.

4. Put together your financial team, composed of an independent financial planner, estate planning attorney, and accountant. Use referrals from trusted people to identify good candidates.
   a. Consider including your children on your financial team, if family relationship dynamics make it reasonable.

5. Build your investment portfolio with your goals in mind, diversifying across multiple investment types (stocks, bonds, mutual funds, alternative investments, etc.) so it will weather short-term fluctuations.
   a. Avoid fad investments, "water cooler" investments, or holding onto underperforming assets for too long.

6. As your portfolio grows more complex over time, periodically revisit it and rebalance as necessary to maintain your risk profile and long-term financial goals.

7. Work with a good estate planning attorney to prepare estate documents, such as a will and trust, which will reduce your tax burden and ensure your assets are distributed according to your wishes.
   a. Identify a trustee who will manage your trust.

8. Consider the legacy you want to leave behind based on your values and mission, then open a dialogue with the next generation and model your values through the actions.

ACKNOWLEDGMENTS

As I look back at my career, there are so many people who were instrumental in the growth of my career, enabling me to eventually fulfill my dream of being in the investment management industry and having my own firm.

First, my wife, Beth, who from the beginning encouraged me and covered all the extra duties at home earlier in my career as my responsibilities required me to be away from home a great deal.

Then, Sam Dekinder and Bob Marchesi, who gave me my first job in the investment industry. I learned a great deal from both of them about researching investments, structuring risk-adjusted portfolios, and managing client relationships. I am not sure I would have achieved my dream without them taking a chance on a young man long on dreams and short on experience.

To my clients, thank you for allowing me to serve you and help you achieve your dreams. I still serve my very first client and have several who have been with me over ten years. Your confidence and dedication to staying on plan are very gratifying and are what keep me going.

To my boys, Steven and Alex. Thanks for understanding while I was away on business and sacrificing during the early years of Providence Financial Advisors. I am blessed to be called your dad and proud of the men you have turned out to be.

I am most grateful to Jesus, my Lord and Savior. He has always been the constant in my life through some very difficult times and tragic events I have endured. Any earthly success is due to His grace and mercy. As Lamentations 3:22–23 states, "The steadfast love of the Lord never ceases; his mercies never come to an end; they are new every morning; great is your faithfulness."

I also want to acknowledge Bill High, who suggested I embark on this journey, and Steven T. Cox Jr., who was a sounding board as I developed the chapters.

Finally, to Jeff Miller and the rest of the team at Streamline Books. They made the task much easier than anticipated. Where were you guys when I was in college?

ABOUT THE AUTHOR

Steven T. Cox founded Providence Financial Advisors LLC to provide individual clients and small businesses with the same level of investment management services and financial planning process enjoyed by larger institutional investors. He observed that technology and product development within the financial industry allowed individuals the same access to many of the same investment disciplines that his institutional clients were utilizing. Since founding the firm, Steve has had the pleasure of working with a variety of clients and helping them achieve their financial goals.

Steve has over thirty-eight years of experience in the investment business. During his career, he has helped clients navigate several market events, including Black Monday in 1987, the booming years of the 1980s and '90s, the financial crisis of 2008, the COVID-19 pandemic, and several other years of volatility.

Prior to founding Providence Financial Advisors LLC, he was a partner in a global investment management firm, representing multiple investment disciplines to clients and investment consultants. Before joining this organization, he was a vice president and consultant for a national investment consulting organization. He was responsible for helping institutional investors develop investment policy, developing asset allocation strategy, conducting investment manager searches, and monitoring investment progress.

Steve achieved the Chartered Financial Analyst (CFA) designation in 1998. He is a member of the CFA Institute and the CFA Society Kansas City, where he currently serves on the board. He also serves on the board of The Salvation Army of Kansas and Western Missouri, and of ReHope, an organization dedicated to helping survivors of sex trafficking rebuild their lives.

Steve loves being "Pops" to his four, soon to be five, grandchildren. He is an avid golfer as well as a Kansas City Chiefs and Royals fan. He and his wife, Beth, love to travel as time permits.

ENDNOTES

1. James Dobson, *Bringing Up Boys: Practical Advice and Encouragement for Those Shaping the Next Generation of Men* (Carol Stream, Ill.: Tyndale Momentum, 2018).

2. Lyle Daly. "What Is the Average Retirement Age in the U.S.?" The Motley Fool, updated March 18, 2024, https://www.fool.com/research/average-retirement-age/.

3. Oddmund Groette, "Day Trading Statistics 2024: The Hard Truth," Quantified Strategies, April 8, 2024, quantifiedstrategies.com/day-trading-statistics/.

4. "Day Trading Risk Disclosure Statement," FINRA (website), accessed July 3, 2024, https://www.finra.org/rules-guidance/rulebooks/finra-rules/2270.

5. Avantis Investors, "The Stories of 2023," December 2023, https://www.avantisinvestors.com/avantis-insights/stories-of-2023/.

6. Avantis Investors, "The Stories of 2023," December 2023, https://www.avantisinvestors.com/avantis-insights/stories-of-2023/.

7. *Guide to Retirement 2024* (J.P. Morgan Asset Management, March 6, 2024), https://am.jpmorgan.com/us/en/asset-management/adv/insights/retirement-insights/guide-to-retirement/.

8.   John Rekenthaler, "The Best US Stock Funds," Morningstar, March 18, 2024, https://www.morningstar.com/columns/rekenthaler-report/ best-us-stock-index-funds.

9.   Morningstar, *Active vs Passive Investing: U.S. Barometer Report*, https://www.morningstar.com/lp/active-passive-barometer.

www.ingramcontent.com/pod-product-compliance
Lightning Source LLC
Chambersburg PA
CBHW030531210326
41597CB00014B/1110